Endless Patterns Coloring Book

ENDLESS PATTERNS COLORING BOOK

Nathan Port

Verdant Publishing

Copyright © 2011 Nathan Port

All rights reserved.

Printed in the United States of America

Verdant Publishing

ISBN: 061548932X
ISBN-13: 978-0615489322

Introduction

Thank you for choosing to spend your time with these designs. Coloring can be a relaxing and enjoyable activity for people of all ages. It can stimulate the imagination and even relieve stress.

Feel free to use your imagination in choosing the colors you use for the designs; however, the use of a color wheel can also aid in choosing pleasing colors.

On a color wheel, red, yellow and blue are the primary colors, and all other colors are formed from the mixture of these. The secondary colors on the color wheel are green, orange and violet, which are formed by the mixture of the primaries. The tertiary colors on the wheel are formed by the mixture of a primary and secondary color, and are yellow-oranage, red-orange, red-violet, blue-violet, blue-green, and yellow-green.

A pleasing color scheme can be chosen by picking three analogous colors- or colors next to each other- on a 12 part color wheel, such as blue-green, green, and blue.

A complementary color scheme is based on colors opposite each other on the color wheel, such as blue and orange.

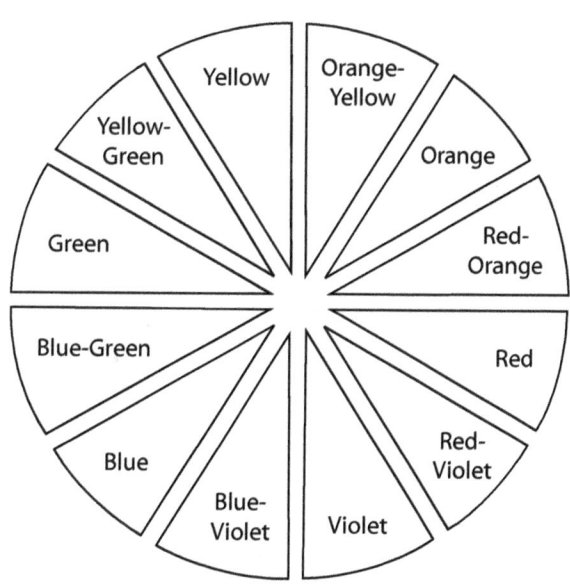

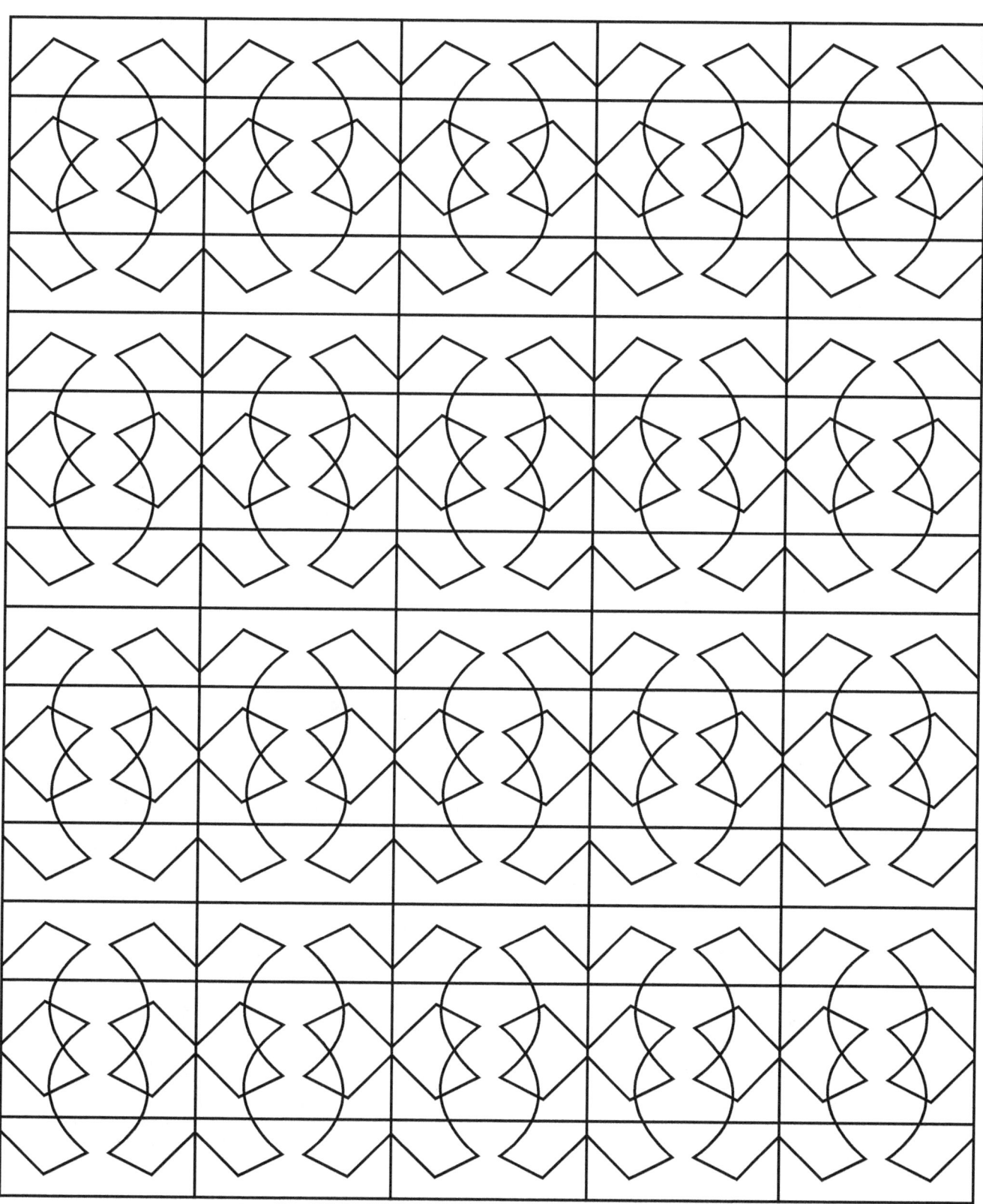

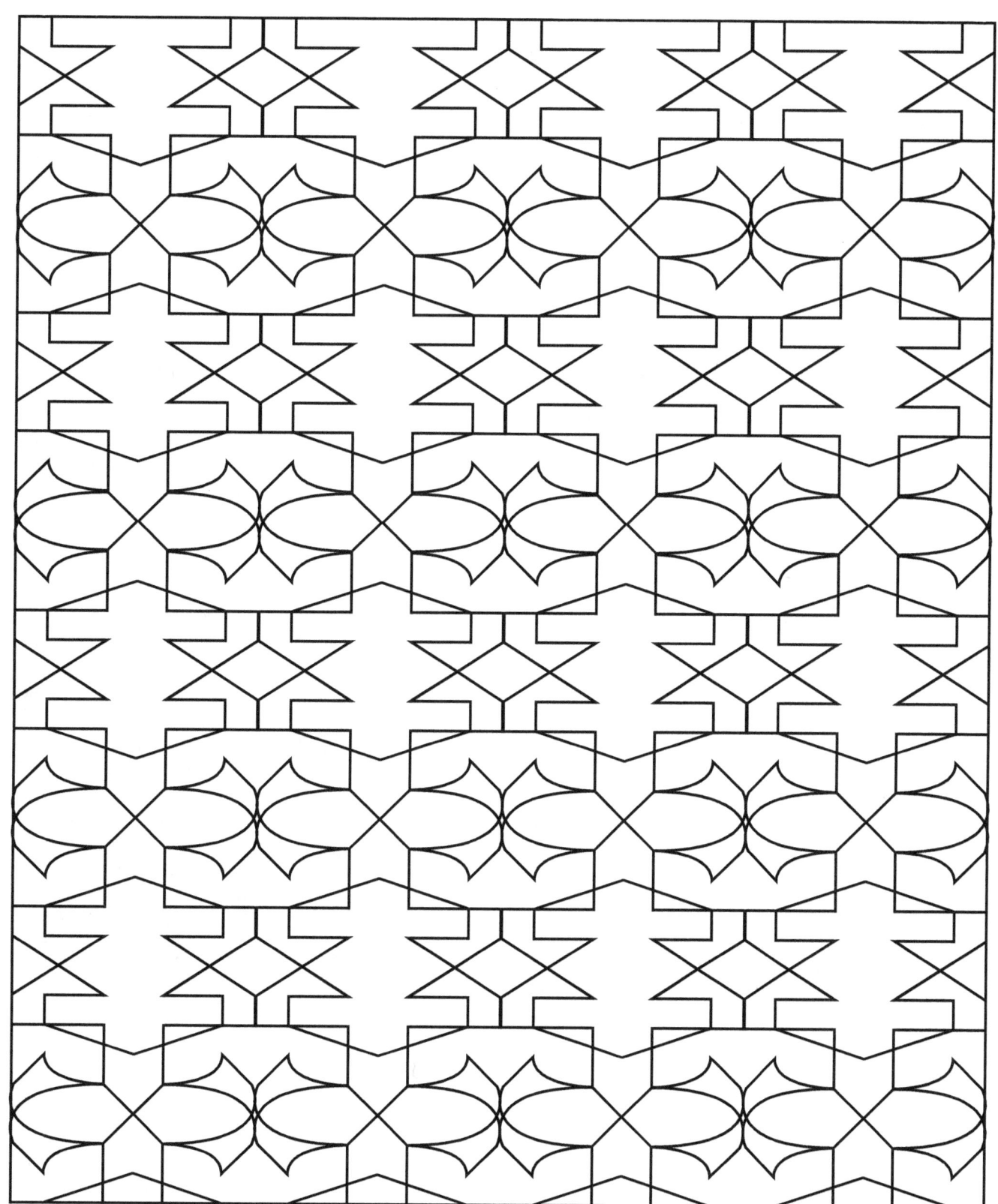

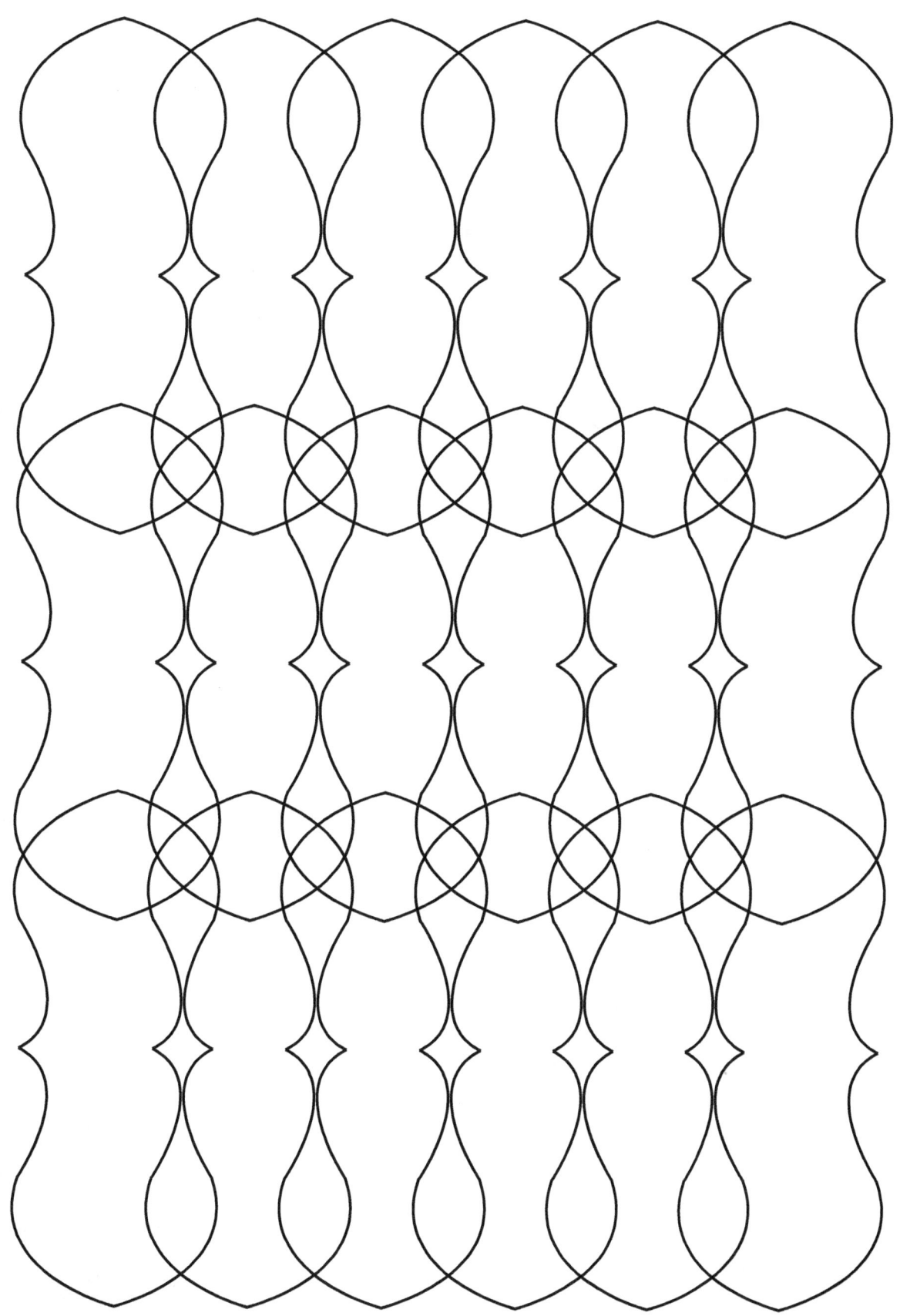

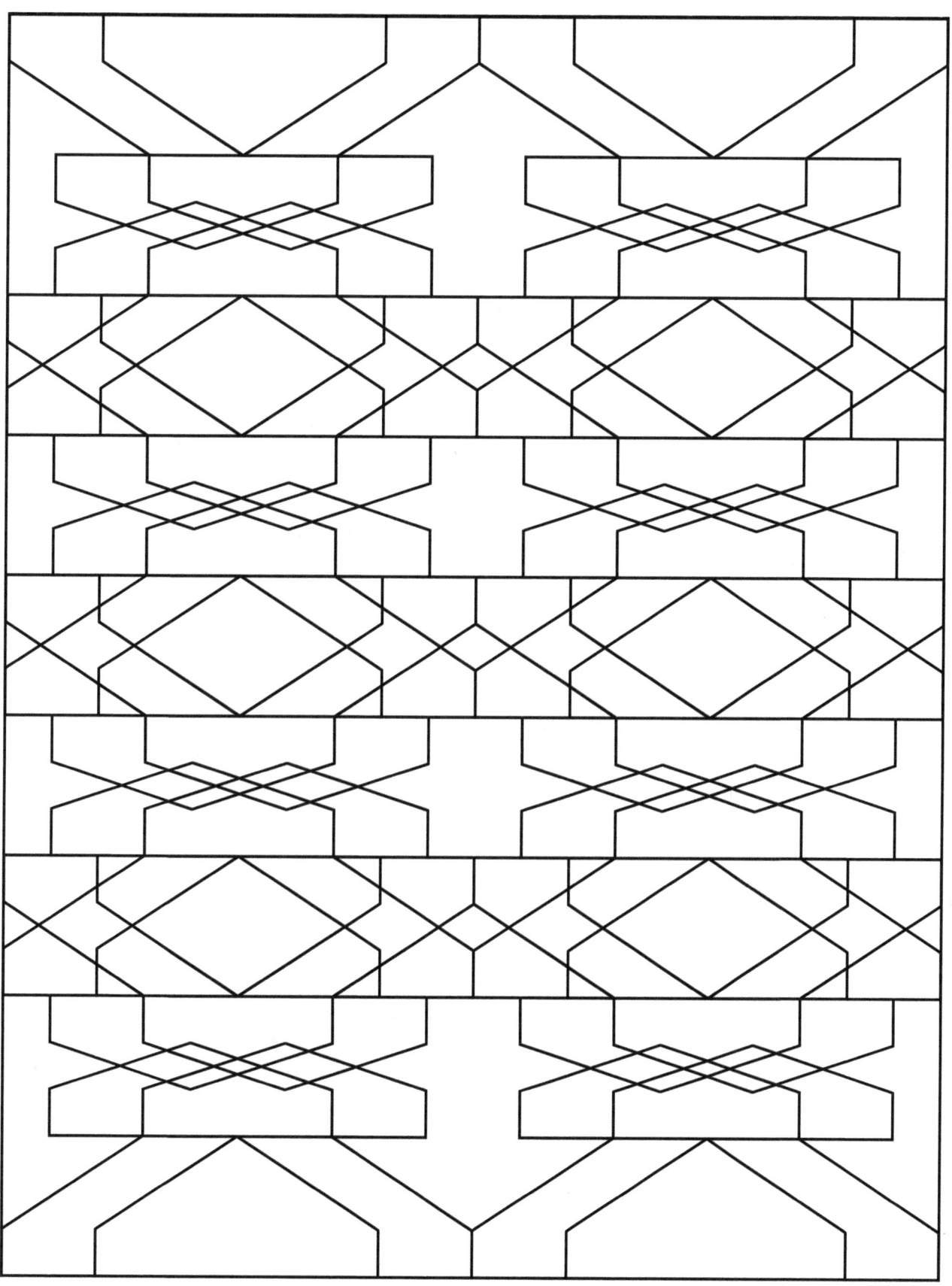

www.ingramcontent.com/pod-product-compliance
Lightning Source LLC
Chambersburg PA
CBHW080528030426
42337CB00023B/4668